FOUR WEEKS IN THE TRENCHES

Fritz Kreisler

FOUR WEEKS IN THE TRENCHES

THE WAR STORY OF A VIOLINIST

BY

FRITZ KREISLER

With Illustrations

Paganiniana Publications, Inc.
211 West Sylvania Avenue
Neptune City, New Jersey 07753

Published by PAGANINIANA PUBLICATIONS, INC.
211 West Sylvania Avenue, Neptune City, N.J. 07753

Kreisler and his wife Harriet

TO MY DEAR WIFE
HARRIET

THE BEST FRIEND
AND STANCHEST COMRADE IN ALL
CIRCUMSTANCES OF LIFE
I DEDICATE THIS LITTLE BOOK
IN HUMBLE TOKEN
OF EVERLASTING GRATITUDE
AND DEVOTION

PREFACE

THIS brief record of the fighting on the Eastern front in the great war is the outcome of a fortunate meeting.

The writer chanced to be dining with Mr. Kreisler soon after his arrival in this country, after his dismissal from the hospital where he recovered from his wound. For nearly two hours he listened, thrilled and moved, to the great violinist's modest, vivid narrative of his experiences and adventures. It seemed in the highest degree desirable that the American public should have an opportunity of reading this narrative from the pen of one in whose art so many of us take a profound interest. It also was apparent that since so little of an authentic nature had been heard from the Russo-Austrian field of warfare, this story would prove an important contribution to the contemporary history of the war.

After much persuasion, Mr. Kreisler reluctantly acceded to the suggestion that he write out his personal memories of the war for publication. He has completed his narrative in the midst of grave difficulties, writing it piecemeal in hotels and railway trains in the course of a concert tour through the country. It is offered by the publishers to the public with confidence that it will be found one of the most absorbing and informing narratives of the war that has yet appeared.

F. G.

FOUR WEEKS IN THE TRENCHES

I

In trying to recall my impressions during my short war duty as an officer in the Austrian Army, I find that my recollections of this period are very uneven and confused. Some of the experiences stand out with absolute clearness; others, however, are blurred. Two or three events which took place in different localities seem merged into one, while in other instances recollection of the chronological order of things is missing. This curious indifference of the memory to values of time and space may be due to the extraordinary physical and mental stress under which the impressions I am trying to chronicle were received. The same state of mind I find is rather characteristic of most people I have met who were in the war. It should not be forgotten, too, that the gigantic upheaval which changed the fundamental condition of life overnight and threatened the very existence of nations naturally dwarfed the individual into nothingness, and the existing interest in the common welfare left practically no room for personal considerations. Then again, at the front, the extreme uncertainty of the morrow tended to lessen the interest in the details of to-day; consequently I may have missed a great many interesting happenings alongside of me which I would have wanted to note under other circumstances. One gets into a strange psychological, almost hypnotic, state of mind while on the firing line which probably prevents the mind's eye from observing and noticing things in a normal way. This accounts, perhaps, for some blank spaces in my memory. Besides, I went out completely resigned to my fate, without much thought for the future. It never occurred to me that I might ever want to write my experiences, and consequently I failed to take notes or to establish certain mnemotechnical landmarks by the aid of which I might now be able to reconstruct all details. I am, therefore, reduced to present an incoherent and rather piecemeal narrative of such episodes as forcibly impressed themselves upon my mind and left an ineradicable mark upon my memory.

The outbreak of the war found my wife and me in Switzerland, where we were taking a cure. On the 31st of July, on opening the paper, I read that the Third Army Corps, to which my regiment (which is stationed in Graz) belonged, had received an order for mobilization.

Although I had resigned my commission as an officer two years before, I immediately left Switzerland, accompanied by my wife, in order to report for duty. As it happened, a wire reached me a day later calling me to the colors.

We went by way of Munich. It was the first day of the declaration of the state of war in Germany. Intense excitement prevailed. In Munich all traffic was stopped; no trains were running except for military purposes. It was only due to the fact that I revealed my intention of rejoining my regiment in Austria that I was able to pass through at all, but by both the civil and military authorities in Bavaria I was shown the greatest posssible consideration and passed through as soon as possible.

We reached Vienna on August first. A startling change had come over the city since I had left it only a few weeks before. Feverish activity everywhere

German officer reading the declaration of war

Kaiser Wilhelm II receiving the acclamation of the people

prevailed. Reservists streamed in by thousands from all parts of the country to report at headquarters. Autos filled with officers whizzed past. Dense crowds surged up and down the streets. Bulletins and extra editions of newspapers passed from hand to hand. Immediately it was evident what a great leveler war is. Differences in rank and social distinctions had practically ceased. All barriers seemed to have fallen; everybody addressed everybody else.

I saw the crowds stop officers of high rank and well-known members of the aristocracy and clergy, also state officials and court functionaries of high rank, in quest of information, which was imparted cheerfully and patiently. The imperial princes could frequently be seen on the Ring Strasse surrounded by cheering crowds or mingling with the public unceremoniously at the cafés, talking to everybody. Of course, the army was idolized. Wherever the troops marched the public broke into cheers and every uniform was the center of an ovation.

While coming from the station I saw two young reservists, to all appearances brothers, as they hurried to the barracks, carrying their small belongings in a valise. Along with them walked a little old lady crying, presumably their mother. They passed a general in full uniform. Up went their hands to their caps in military salute, whereupon the old general threw his arms wide open and embraced them both, saying: "Go on, my boys, do your duty bravely and stand firm for your emperor and your country. God willing, you will come back to your old mother." The old lady smiled through her tears. A shout went up, and the crowds surrounding the general cheered him. Long after I had left I could hear them shouting.

A few streets farther on I saw in an open café a young couple, a reservist in field uniform and a young girl, his bride or sweetheart. They sat there, hands linked, utterly oblivious of their surroundings and of the world at large. When somebody in the crowd espied them, a great shout went up, the public rushing to the table and surrounding them, then breaking into applause and waving hats and handkerchiefs. At first the young couple seemed to be utterly taken aback and only slowly did they realize that the ovation was meant for them. They seemed confused, the young girl blushing and hiding her face in her hands, the young man rising to his feet, saluting and bowing. More cheers and applause. He opened his mouth as if wanting to speak. There was a sudden silence. He was vainly struggling for expression, but then his face lit up as if by inspiration. Standing erect, hand at his cap, in a pose of military salute, he intoned the Austrian national hymn. In a second every head in that throng was bared. All traffic suddenly stopped, everybody, passengers as well as conductors of the cars, joining in the anthem. The neighboring windows soon filled with people, and soon it was a chorus of thousands of voices. The volume of tone and the intensity of feeling seemed to raise the inspiring anthem to the uttermost heights of sublime majesty. We were then on our way to the station, and long afterwards we could hear the singing, swelling like a human organ.

What impressed me particularly in Vienna was the strict order everywhere. No mob disturbances of any kind, in spite of the greatly increased liberty and relaxation of police regulations. Nor was there any runaway chauvinism noticeable, aside from the occasional singing of patriotic songs and demon-

Kreisler's battalion taking oath at Leoben

A group of officers and their wives at Leoben

strations like the one I just described. The keynote of popular feeling was quiet dignity, joined to determination, with an undercurrent of solemn gravity and responsibility.

I had stopped in Vienna only long enough to bid good-bye to my father, and left for the headquarters of my regiment in Graz. I reported there for duty and then went to join the Fourth Battalion, which was stationed at Leoben, one hour away from Graz, my orders being to take command of the first platoon in the sixteenth company. My platoon consisted of fifty-five men, two buglers, and an ambulance patrol of four.

In Leoben my wife and I remained a week, which was spent in organizing, equipping, requisitioning, recruiting, and preliminary drilling. These were happy days, as we officers met for the first time, friendships and bonds being sealed which subsequently were tested in common danger and amidst privation and stress. Many of the officers had brought their wives and soon delightful intercourse, utterly free from formality, developed, without any regard or reference to rank, wealth, or station in private life. Among the reserve officers of my battalion were a famous sculptor, a well-known philologist, two university professors (one of mathematics, the other of natural science), a prince, and a civil engineer at the head of one of the largest Austrian steel corporations. The surgeon of our battalion was the head of a great medical institution and a man of international fame. Among my men in the platoon were a painter, two college professors, a singer of repute, a banker, and a post official of high rank. But nobody cared and in fact I myself did not know until much later what distinguished men were in my platoon. A great cloak of brotherhood seemed to

Kreisler playing at a Red Cross benefit at Leoben

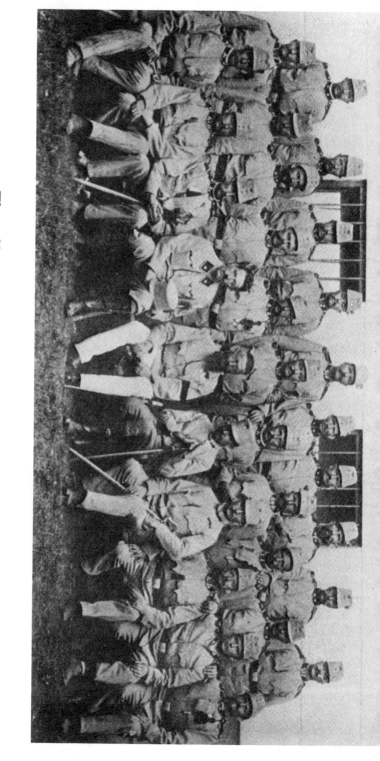

The officers and surgeon of Kreisler's company

have enveloped everybody and everything, even differences in military rank
not being so obvious at this time, for the
officers made friends of their men, and
in turn were worshiped by them.

My wife volunteered her services as
Red Cross nurse, insisting upon being
sent to the front, in order to be as near
me as could be, but it developed later
that no nurse was allowed to go farther
than the large troop hospitals far in the
rear of the actual operations. Upon my
urgent appeal she desisted and remained
in Vienna after I had left, nursing in the
barracks, which are now used for hospital work. In fact, almost every third
or fourth house, both private and public, as well as schools, were given to the
use of the government and converted
into Red Cross stations.

The happy days in Leoben came to an
abrupt end, my regiment receiving orders to start immediately for the front.

We proceeded to Graz, where we joined the other three battalions and were entrained for an unknown destination. We traveled via Budapest to Galicia, and left the train at Strij, a very important railroad center south of Lemberg. It must be understood that the only reports reaching us from the fighting line at that time were to the effect that the Russians had been driven back from our border, and that the Austrian armies actually stood on the enemy's soil. Strij being hundreds of miles away from the Russian frontier, we could not but surmise that we were going to be stationed there some time for the purpose of training and maneuvering. This belief was strengthened by the fact that our regiment belonged to the Landsturm, or second line of reserves, originally intended for home service. We were, however, alarmed that very same night and marched out of Strij for a distance of about twenty miles, in conjunction with the entire Third Army Corps. After a short pause for the purpose of eating and feeding the horses, we marched another twenty-two miles. This first day's march constituted a very strong test of endurance in consequence of our comparative softness and lack of training, especially as, in addition to his heavy rifle, bayonet, ammunition, and spade, each soldier was burdened with a knapsack containing emergency provisions in the form of tinned meats, coffee extract, sugar, salt, rice, and biscuits, together with various tin cooking and eating utensils; furthermore a second pair of shoes, extra blouse, changes of underwear, etc. On top of this heavy pack a winter overcoat and part of a tent were strapped, the entire weight of the equipment being in the neighborhood of fifty pounds.

The day wore on. Signs of fatigue

soon manifested themselves more and more strongly, and slowly the men dropped out one by one, from sheer exhaustion. No murmur of complaint, however, would be heard. Most of those who fell out of line, after taking a breathing space for a few minutes, staggered on again. The few that remained behind joined the regiment later on when camp was established. We wondered then at the necessity of such a forced march, being unable to see a reason for it, unless it was to put us in training.

Night had fallen when we reached a small monastery in the midst of a forest, where the peaceful surroundings and the monastic life, entirely untouched by the war fever, seemed strange indeed. Camp was established, tents erected, fires were lighted, and coffee made. Soon a life of bustling activity sprang up in the wilderness, in the midst of the forest which only a few hours before had been deserted.

Soldiers in full battle gear

Troops on the move

It made a weird and impressive picture in the wonderful starlight night, these soldiers sitting around the camp fires softly singing in chorus; the fantastic outlines of the monastery half hidden in the woods; the dark figures of the monks moving silently back and forth amongst the shadows of the trees as they brought refreshments to the troops; the red glow of the camp fires illuminating the eager and enthusiastic faces of the young officers grouped around the colonel; the snorting and stamping of the horses nearby; an occasional melodic outcry of a sentinel out in the night; all these things merging into an unforgettable scene of great romanticism and beauty. That night I lay for a long while stretched near the smoldering ashes of the camp fire, with my cape as a blanket, in a state of lassitude and somnolence, my soul filled with exaltation and happiness over the beauty around me.

The rest, however, was of very short duration, for at six o'clock in the morning we were aroused, camp was broken up and soon afterwards we started on a forced march of twenty-two miles without a halt, during which we twice had to wade knee-deep through rivers. By midday most of the men were so exhausted that they could hardly crawl along. It was remarkable that the comparatively weaker and more refined city-bred people who had done little physical work in their lives, most of them being professional men, withstood hardships better than the sturdy and, to all appearances, stronger peasants. The only explanation for it being perhaps that the city-bred people, in consequence of their better surroundings and by reason of their education, had more will power and nervous strength than the peasants.

At half-past two we reached a clearing in the midst of a wood through which a river flowed. Here camp was again established and a half hour later all the hardships of the march were once more forgotten in the bustle of camp life. This time we had a full rest until the next morning at four o'clock, when suddenly orders for marching were given. After we had been under way for about three hours we heard far-away, repeated rumbling which sounded like distant thunder. Not for a moment did we associate it with cannonading, being, as we supposed, hundreds of miles away from the nearest place where Russians could possibly be. Suddenly a mounted ordnance officer came rushing with a message to our colonel. We came to a halt and all officers were summoned to the colonel who, addressing us in his usual quiet, almost businesslike way, said: "Gentlemen, accept my congratulations, I have good news for you, we may meet the enemy to-day and I sincerely hope to lead you to the fight before evening." We were thunderstruck at the sudden realization that the Russians had penetrated so deeply into Galicia. The despondency which followed this startling revelation, however, was quickly replaced by the intense excitement of meeting the enemy so soon. We hurried back to our companies, imparting the news to the men, who broke forth into shouts of enthusiasm. All the fatigue so plainly noticeable only a few minutes before, suddenly vanished as if by magic, and every one seemed alert, springy, and full of spirit. We energetically resumed the march in the direction of the distant rumbling, which indicated that the artillery of our advance guard had engaged the enemy. My regiment then was part of the main body of a division. A second division advanced on the road parallel to ours, about a mile and a quarter to our left. Both columns belonged to the Third Army

Corps and kept up constant communication with each other through mounted dispatch bearers and motor cycles.

The cannonading had meanwhile come perceptibly nearer, and in the midst of the dense forest we again came to a short halt. Orders were given to load rifles, and upon emerging from the woods we fell into open formation, the men marching abreast, the companies at a distance of three hundred yards, with the battalions at a distance of about a thousand yards. We were slowly entering the range of the Russian artillery. About a mile ahead we could see numbers of harmless looking round clouds, looking like ringlets of smoke from a huge cigar, indicating the places where shrapnel had exploded in mid-air. Our men, not being familiar with the spectacle, took no notice of it, but we officers knew its significance, and I daresay many a heart beat as wildly as mine did.

We marched on until the command was given for us to deploy, and soon afterwards the first shrapnel whizzed over our heads. It did no harm, nor did the second and third, but the fourth hit three men in the battalion in the rear of us. Our forward movement, however, was not interrupted, and we did not see or hear anything beyond two or three startled cries. The next shell burst right ahead of us, sending a shower of bullets and steel fragments around. A man about twenty yards to the right of my company, but not of my platoon, leaped into the air with an agonizing cry and fell in a heap, mortally wounded. As we were advancing very swiftly, I only saw it as in a dream, while running by. Then came in rapid succession four or five terrific explosions right over our heads, and I felt a sudden gust of cold wind strike my cheek as a big shell fragment came howling through the air, ploughing the ground viciously as it struck and sending a spray of sand around.

We ran on perhaps a quarter of a mile, when from the rear came the sharp command, "Down," and the next second we lay on the ground, panting and exhausted, my heart almost bursting with the exertion. Simultaneously the whizzing of a motor above our heads could be heard and we knew why the enemy's shrapnel had so suddenly found us. It was a Russian aeroplane which presumably had signaled our approach, together with the range, to the Russian gunners, and now was probably directing their fire and closely watching its effect, for a chain of hills was hiding us from the view of the enemy, who consequently had to fire indirectly. The air craft hovered above our heads, but we were forbidden to fire at it, the extremely difficult, almost vertical aim promising little success, aside from the danger of our bullets falling back among us. Our reserves in the rear had apparently sighted the air craft too, for soon we heard a volley of rifle fire from that direction and simultaneously the aeroplane arose and disappeared in the clouds.

Just then our own artillery came thundering up, occupied a little hill in the rear and opened fire on the enemy. The moral effect of the thundering of one's own artillery is most extraordinary, and many of us thought that we had never heard any more welcome sound than the deep roaring and crashing that started in at our rear. It quickly helped to disperse the nervousness caused by the first entering into battle and to restore self control and confidence. Besides, by getting into action, our artillery was now focusing the attention and drawing the fire of the Russian guns, for most of the latter's shells whined harmlessly above us, being aimed at the batteries in our

Laying down an artillery barrage

An attack through the fields

rear. Considerably relieved by this diversion, we resumed our forward movement after about fifteen minutes of further rest, our goal being the little chain of hills which our advance guard had previously occupied pending our arrival. Here we were ordered to take up positions and dig trenches, any further advance being out of the question, as the Russian artillery overlooked and commanded the entire plain stretching in front of us.

We started at once to dig our trenches, half of my platoon stepping forward abreast, the men being placed an arm's length apart. After laying their rifles down, barrels pointing to the enemy, a line was drawn behind the row of rifles and parallel to it. Then each man would dig up the ground, starting from his part of the line backwards, throwing forward the earth removed, until it formed a sort of breastwork. The second half of the platoon was meanwhile resting in the rear, rifle in hand and ready for action. After a half hour they took the place of the first division at work, and vice versa. Within an hour work on the trenches was so far advanced that they could be deepened while standing in them. Such an open trench affords sufficient shelter against rifle bullets striking from the front and can be made in a measure shell proof by being covered with boards, if at hand, and with sod.

In the western area of the theater of war, in France and Flanders, where whole armies were deadlocked, facing each other for weeks without shifting their position an inch, such trenches become an elaborate affair, with extensive underground working and wing connections of lines which almost constitute little fortresses and afford a certain measure of comfort. But where we were in Galicia at the beginning of the war, with conditions utterly unsteady and positions shifting daily and hourly, only the most superficial trenches were used. In fact, we thought ourselves fortunate if we could requisition enough straw to cover the bottom. That afternoon we had about half finished our work when our friend the aeroplane appeared on the horizon again. This time we immediately opened fire. It disappeared, but apparently had seen enough, for very soon our position was shelled. By this time, however, shrapnel had almost ceased to be a source of concern to us and we scarcely paid any attention to it. Human nerves quickly get accustomed to the most unusual conditions and circumstances and I noticed that quite a number of men actually fell asleep from sheer exhaustion in the trenches, in spite of the roaring of the cannon about us and the whizzing of shrapnel over our heads.

I, too, soon got accustomed to the

deadly missiles, — in fact, I had already started to make observations of their peculiarities. My ear, accustomed to differentiate sounds of all kinds, had some time ago, while we still advanced, noted a remarkable discrepancy in the peculiar whine produced by the different shells in their rapid flight through the air as they passed over our heads, some sounding shrill, with a rising tendency, and the others rather dull, with a falling cadence. A short observation revealed the fact that the passing of a dull- sounding shell was invariably preceded by a flash from one of our own cannon in the rear on the hill, which conclusively proved it to be an Austrian shell. It must be understood that as we were advancing between the positions of the Austrian and Russian artillery, both kinds of shells were passing over our heads. As we advanced the difference between shrill and dull shell grew less and less perceptible, until I could hardly tell them apart. Upon nearing the hill the difference increased again more and more until on the hill itself it was very marked. After our trench was finished I crawled to the top of the hill until I could make out the flash of the Russian guns on the opposite heights and by timing flash and actual passing of the shell, found to my astonishment that now the Russian missiles had become dull, while on the other hand, the shrill shell was invariably heralded by a flash from one of our guns, now far in the rear. What had happened was this: Every shell describes in its course a parabolic line, with the first half of the curve ascending and the second one descending. Apparently in the first half of its curve, that is, its course while ascending, the shell produced a dull whine accompanied by a falling cadence, which changes to a rising shrill as soon as the acme has been reached and the curve points downward again. The acme for both kinds of shells naturally was exactly the half distance between the Russian and Austrian artillery and this was the point where I had noticed that the difference was the least marked. A few days later, in talking over my observation with an artillery officer, I was told the fact was known that the shells sounded different going up than when coming down, but this knowledge was not used for practical purposes. When I told him that I could actually determine by the sound the exact place where a shell coming from the opposing batteries was reaching its acme, he thought that this would be of great value in a case where the position of the opposing battery was hidden and thus could be located. He apparently spoke to his commander about me, for a few days later I was sent on a reconnoitering tour, with the object of marking on the map the exact spot where I thought the hostile shells were reaching their acme, and it was later on reported to me that I had succeeded in giving to our batteries the almost exact range of the Russian guns. I have gone into this matter at some length, because it is the only instance where my musical ear was of value during my service.

To return to my narrative, the losses which my battalion suffered that day seemed extraordinarily small when compared with the accuracy of the Russian artillery's aim and the number of missiles they fired. I counted seventy-four shrapnel that burst in a circle of half a mile around us in about two hours, and yet we had no more than about eighteen casualties. The most difficult part was to lie still and motionless while death was being dealt all about us, and it was then and there that I had my first experience of seeing death next to me. A soldier of my platoon, while digging in the trench, suddenly leaned back, began to cough like an old man, a little blood broke from his lips, and he crumpled together in a heap and lay quite still. I could not realize that this was the end, for his eyes were wide open and his face wore the stamp of complete serenity. Apparently he had not suffered at all. The man had been a favorite with all his fellows by reason of his good humor, and that he was now stretched out dead seemed unbelievable. I saw a great many men die afterwards, some suffering horribly, but I do not recall any death that affected me quite so much as that of this first victim in my platoon.

Soldiers killed in battle

Kreisler, after three weeks at the front

II

THE artillery duel died out with the coming of darkness and we settled down to rest, half of the men taking watch while the others slept. At five o'clock in the morning our regiment suddenly received the order to fall in, and, together with two other regiments, was drawn out of the fighting line. Our commanding general had received news that an isolated detachment on the extreme right wing of our army, about fifteen miles east of us, had been entirely surrounded by a strong Russian body, and we were ordered to relieve them. It must not be forgotten that our men had been under a most incredible strain for the last three days with barely any rest during the nights and not more than one meal a day. They had actually welcomed entering the firing line, as a relief from the fatigues of marching with their heavy burdens. It is curious how indifferent one becomes to danger if one's organism is worn down and brain and faculty of perception numbed by physical exertion. It was, therefore, with badly broken-down strength that we started on this relief expedition, and it was good to see how unflinchingly the soldiers undertook their unexpected new task. All we had to say to our men was: "Boys, your brothers are needing you. They are cut off from all possible relief unless you bring it. Their lives are at stake, and as they are defending one of the most strategically important points — the right wing of our army — you can turn the tide of the whole battle in our favor; so go on." And on they went, staggering and stumbling, and at the end of a few hours almost crawling, but ever forward.

Suddenly we came up with another

regiment which had been called to the same task, and the colonel of the new regiment, being older in rank than our colonel, took command of the newly formed brigade of two regiments. My company happened to march at the head of the regiment and the new brigadier rode for some time alongside of me. I was deeply impressed by his firm military and yet unassuming bearing and his deep glowing enthusiasm for his army and his men. He told me with pride that two of his sons were serving in the army, too, one as an artillery officer and the other one as an officer with the sappers. We were then approaching the point where we could hear distinctly the fire of our own batteries and the answer from the Russians, and here and there a volley of rifle fire. Our colonel urged us on to renewed energy, and knowledge that we were nearing our goal seemed to give new strength to our men. Already we were witnessing evidences of the first fight that had passed here, for wounded men constantly passed us on stretchers. Suddenly I saw the face of the colonel riding next to me, light up with excitement as a wounded man was borne past. He addressed a few words to the stretcher-bearers and then turned to me, saying: "The regiment of my son is fighting on the hill. It is one of their men they have brought by." He urged us on again, and it seemed to me as if I noticed — or was it my imagination — a new note of appeal in his face. Suddenly another stretcher was brought past. The colonel at my side jumped from his horse, crying out, "My boy," and a feeble voice answered, "Father." We all stopped as if a command had been given, to look at the young officer who lay on the stretcher, his eyes all aglow with enthusiasm and joy, unmindful of his own wound as he cried out, "Father, how splendid that the relief should just come from you! Go on. We held out splendidly. All we need is ammunition and a little moral support. Go on, don't stop for me, I am all right." The old colonel stood like a statue of bronze. His face had become suddenly ashen gray. He looked at the doctor and tried to catch his expression. The doctor seemed grave. But the young man urged us on, saying, "Go on, go on, I'll be all right to-morrow." The whole incident had not lasted more than five minutes, barely longer than it takes to write it. The colonel mounted his horse, sternly commanding us to march forward, but the light had died out of his eyes.

Within the next ten minutes a hail of shrapnel was greeting us, but hardly any one of us was conscious of it, so terribly and deeply were we affected by the scene of tragedy that had just been enacted before us. I remember foolishly mumbling something to the silent man riding next to me, something about the power of recuperation of youth, about the comparative harmlessness of the pointed, steelmantled rifle bullets which on account of their terrific percussion make small clean wounds and rarely cause splintering of the bone or blood poisoning. I remember saying that I had quite a medical knowledge and that it seemed to me that his son was not mortally wounded. But he knew better. He never said a word, only, a few minutes later, "He *was* my only hope"; and I can't express how ominous that word "was" sounded to me. But just then the command to deploy was given and the excitement that followed drowned for the time being all melancholy thoughts.

We quickly ascended the hill where the isolated detachment of Austrians had kept the Russians at bay for fully twenty-four hours and opened fire on the enemy, while the second regiment tried to turn his left flank. The Russians slowly fell back but we followed them, and a sort of running fight ensued, during which my regiment lost about fifty — dead and wounded. The Russians temporarily resisted again, but soon the pressure from our other regiment on their flank began to be felt and they fled rather disorderly, leaving two machine guns, some ammunition, and four carriages full of provisions in our hands, while the regiment which had executed the flanking movement took two hundred and forty prisoners.

Around eight o'clock at night the fight was stopped for want of light, and we took up our newly acquired positions, entrenched them well, and began to make ready for the night. Orders for outpost duty were given and the officers were again called to the brigadier-colonel, who in a few words outlined the situation to us, thanking us for the pertinacity and bravery shown by the troops, and adding that the success of the expedition lay in the fact that we had arrived in time to save the situation.

Then the question of transporting prisoners to the rear came up, and while the brigadier's eyes were searching us I felt that he was going to entrust me with that mission. He looked at me, gave me the order in a short, measured way, but his eyes gazed searchingly and deeply into mine, and I thought I understood the unspoken message. So, tired as I was, I immediately set out with a guard of twenty men to transport the two hundred and forty Russian prisoners, among whom were two officers, back behind the fighting line. They seemed not unhappy over their lot — in fact, were smoking and chatting freely while we marched back. One of the Russian officers had a wound in his leg and was carried on a stretcher, but he, too, seemed quite at ease, conversing with me in French and congratulating me upon the bravery our isolated detachment had shown against the terrific onslaught. As soon as I had delivered them safely into the hands of the commander of our reserves, I inquired the way to the nearest field hospital in search of the young officer, the son of our brigadier-colonel. It was then about nine o'clock at night, and on entering the peasant's hut where the field hospital was established, I saw at a glance that I had come too late. He lay there still, hands folded over his breast with as serene and happy an expression as if asleep. His faithful orderly sat weeping next to him, and some kind hand had laid a small bunch of field flowers on his breast.

From the doctor I got the full information. He had received a shot in the abdomen and a rifle bullet had grazed his cheek. His last words had been a fervent expression of joy over the relief brought by his father and the knowledge that the position would not be taken by the Russians. He had died as simply as a child, without regret, and utterly happy. I took the orderly with me, asking him to carry all the belongings of the young officer with him in order to transmit them to his father.

When I returned with the orderly, the brigadier was issuing orders to his officers and conferring with them about the military situation. He saw me come, yet not a muscle moved in his face, nor did he interrupt his conversation. I was overwhelmed by the power this man showed at that minute, and admit I had not the courage to break the news to him, but it was unnecessary, for he understood. The faithful orderly stepped forward, as I had bidden him, presenting to the old man the pocketbook and small articles that belonged to his son. While he did so he broke forth into sobs, lamenting aloud the loss of his beloved lieutenant, yet not a muscle moved in the face of the father. He took my report, nodded curtly, dismissed me without a word, and turned back to his ordnance officers, resuming the conversation.

I assumed the command of my platoon which in the mean time had been assigned to do some outpost duty under the command of the sergeant. I inquired about their position and went out to join them. About midnight we were relieved, and when marching back, passed the place where the tent of the brigadier had been erected. I saw a dark figure lying on the floor, seemingly in deep sleep, and ordering my men to march on I crept silently forward. Then I saw that his shoulders were convulsively shaking and I knew that the mask of iron had fallen at last. The night was chilly so I entered his tent in search of his overcoat and laid it around his shoulders. He never noticed it. The next morning when I saw him his face was as immovable as it had been the night before, but he seemed to have aged by many years.

The next day was a comparatively restful one. We fortified the entrenchments which we had taken, and as our battle lines were extended to the right, from being the extreme right we became almost the center of the new position which extended for perhaps ten miles from northwest to southeast about eighteen miles south of Lemberg.

The next few days were given to repairs, provisioning, and resting, with occasional small skirmishes and shifting of positions. Then one night a scouting aeroplane brought news of a forward movement of about five Russian army corps, which seemed to push in the direction of our center. Against this force we could muster only about two army corps, but our strategical position seemed a very good one, both the extreme flanks of our army being protected by large and impassable swamps. Evidently the Russians had realized the impossibility of turning our flanks and were endeavoring to pierce our center by means of a vigorous frontal attack, relying upon their great superiority in numbers. Every preparation had been made to meet the onslaught during the night. Our trenches had been strengthened, the artillery had been brought into position, cleverly masked by means of transplanted bushes, the field in front of us had been cleared of objects obstructing the view, and the sappers had been feverishly busy constructing formidable barbed-wire entanglements and carefully measuring the shooting distances, marking the different ranges by bundles of hay or other innocent-looking objects, which were placed here and there in the field.

At nine o'clock in the morning everything was ready to receive the enemy, the men taking a short and well-deserved rest in their trenches, while we officers were called to the colonel, who acquainted us with the general situation, and, giving his orders, addressed us in a short, business-like way, appealing to our sense of duty and expressing his firm belief in our victory. We all knew that his martial attitude and abrupt manner were a mask to hide his inner self, full of throbbing emotion and tender solicitude for his subordinates, and we returned to our trenches deeply moved.

The camp was absolutely quiet. The only movements noticeable being around the field kitchens in the rear, which were being removed from the battle line. A half hour later any casual observer, glancing over the deserted fields might have laughed at the intimation that the earth around him was harboring thousands of men armed to their teeth, and that pandemonium of hell would break loose within an hour. Barely a sound was audible, and a hush of expectancy descended upon us. I looked around at my men in the trench; some were quietly asleep, some writing letters, others conversed in subdued and hushed tones. Every face I saw bore the unmistakable stamp of the feeling so characteristic of the last hour before a battle, — that curious mixture of solemn dignity, grave responsibility, and suppressed emotion, with an undercurrent of sad resignation. They were pondering over their possible fate, or perhaps dreaming of their dear ones at home.

By and by even the little conversation ceased, and they sat quite silent, waiting and waiting, perhaps awed by their own silence. Sometimes one would bravely try to crack a joke, and they laughed, but it sounded strained. They were plainly nervous, these brave men that fought like lions in the open when led to an attack, heedless of danger and destruction. They felt under a cloud in the security of the trenches, and they were conscious of it and ashamed. Sometimes my faithful orderly would turn his eye on me, mute, as if in quest of an explanation of his own feeling. Poor dear unsophisticated boy! I was as nervous as they all were, although trying my best to look unconcerned; but I knew that the hush that hovered around us like a dark cloud would give way like magic to wild enthusiasm as soon as the first shot broke the spell and the exultation of the battle took hold of us all.

Suddenly, at about ten o'clock, a dull thud sounded somewhere far away from us, and simultaneously we saw a small white round cloud about half a mile ahead of us where the shrapnel had exploded. The battle had begun. Other shots followed shortly, exploding here and there, but doing no harm. The Russian gunners evidently were trying to locate and draw an answer from our batteries. These, however, remained mute, not caring to reveal their position. For a long time the Russians fired at random, mostly at too short a range to do any harm, but slowly the harmless-looking white clouds came nearer, until a shell, whining as it whizzed past us, burst about a hundred yards behind our trench. A second shell followed, exploding almost at the same place. At the same time, we noticed a faint spinning noise above us. Soaring high above our position, looking like a speck in the firmament, flew a Russian aeroplane, watching the effect of the shells and presumably directing the fire of the Russian artillery. This explained its sudden accuracy. One of our aeroplanes rose, giving chase to the enemy, and simultaneously our batteries got into action. The Russians kept up a sharply concentrated, well-directed fire against our center, our gunners responding gallantly, and the spirited artillery duel which ensued grew in intensity until the entrails of the earth seemed fairly to shake with the thunder.

By one o'clock the incessant roaring, crashing, and splintering of bursting shells had become almost unendurable to our nerves, which were already strained to the snapping-point by the lack of action and the expectancy. Suddenly there appeared a thin dark line on the horizon which moved rapidly towards us, looking not unlike a huge running bird with immense outstretched wings. We looked through our field glasses; there could be no doubt, — it was Russian cavalry, swooping down upon us with incredible impetus and swiftness. I quickly glanced at our colonel. He stared open-mouthed. This was, indeed, good fortune for us, — too good to believe. No cavalry attack could stand before well-disciplined infantry, providing the latter keep cool and well composed, calmly waiting until the riders come sufficiently close to take sure aim.

There was action for us at last. At a sharp word of command, our men scrambled out of the trenches for better view and aim, shouting with joy as they did so. What a change had come over us all! My heart beat with wild exultation. I glanced at my men. They were all eagerness and determination, hand at the trigger, eyes on the approaching enemy, every muscle strained, yet calm, their bronzed faces hardened into immobility, waiting for the command to fire. Every subaltern officer's eye hung on our colonel, who stood about thirty yards ahead of us on a little hill, his figure well defined in the sunlight, motionless, the very picture of calm assurance and proud bearing. He scanned the horizon with his glasses. Shrapnel was hailing around him, but he seemed utterly unaware of it; for that matter we had all forgotten it, though it kept up its terrible uproar, spitting here and there destruction into our midst.

By this time the avalanche of tramping horses had come perceptibly nearer. Soon they would sweep by the bundle of hay which marked the carefully measured range within which our fire was terribly effective. Suddenly the mad stampede came to an abrupt standstill, and then the Cossacks scattered precipitately to the right and left, only to disclose in their rear the advancing Russian infantry, the movements of which it had been their endeavor to veil.

The infantry moved forward in loose

lines, endlessly rolling on like shallow waves overtaking each other, one line running forward, then suddenly disappearing by throwing itself down and opening fire on us to cover the advance of the other line, and so on, while their artillery kept up a hellish uproar spreading destruction through our lines. Simultaneously a Russian aeroplane swept down upon us with a noise like an angered bird of prey and pelted us with bombs, the effects of which, however, were more moral than actual, for we had regained the security of the trenches and opened fire on the approaching enemy, who in spite of heavy losses advanced steadily until he reached our wire entanglements. There he was greeted by a deadly fire from our machine guns. The first Russian lines were mowed down as if by a gigantic scythe, and so were the reserves as they tried to advance. The first attack had collapsed. After a short time, however, they came on again, this time more cautiously, armed with nippers to cut the barbed wire and using the bodies of their own fallen comrades as a rampart. Again they were repulsed. Once more their cavalry executed a feigned attack under cover of which the Russian infantry rallied, strongly reinforced by reserves, and more determined than ever.

Supported by heavy artillery fire their lines rolled endlessly on and hurled themselves against the barbed-wire fences. For a short time it almost seemed, as if they would break through by sheer weight of numbers. At that critical moment, however, our reserves succeeded in executing a flanking movement. Surprised and caught in a deadly cross-fire, the Russian line wavered and finally they fled in disorder.

All these combined artillery, infantry, cavalry, and aeroplane attacks had utterly failed in their object of dislodging our center or shaking its position, each one being frustrated by the resourceful, cool alertness of our commanding general and the splendid heroism and stoicism of our troops. But the strain of the continuous fighting for nearly the whole day without respite of any kind, or chance for food or rest, in the end told on the power of endurance of our men, and when the last attack had been successfully repulsed they lay mostly prostrated on the ground, panting and exhausted. Our losses had been very considerable, too, stretcher-bearers being busy administering first aid and carrying the wounded back to the nearest field hospital, while many a brave man lay stark and still.

By eight o'clock it had grown perceptibly cooler. We now had time to collect our impressions and look about us. The Russians had left many dead on the field, and at the barbed-wire entanglements which our sappers had constructed as an obstacle to their advance, their bodies lay heaped upon each other, looking not unlike the more innocent bundles of hay lying in the field. We could see the small Red Cross parties in the field climbing over the horribly grotesque tumuli of bodies, trying to disentangle the wounded from the dead and administer first aid to them.

Enthusiasm seemed suddenly to disappear before this terrible spectacle. Life that only a few hours before had glowed with enthusiasm and exultation, suddenly paled and sickened. The silence of the night was interrupted only by the low moaning of the wounded that came regularly to us. It was hideous in its terrible monotony. The moon had risen, throwing fantastic lights and shadows over the desolate landscape and the heaped-up dead. These grotesque piles

Russian casualties

The dead awaiting burial

of human bodies seemed like a monstrous sacrificial offering immolated on the altar of some fiendishly cruel, antique deity. I felt faint and sick at heart and near swooning away. I lay on the floor for some time unconscious of what was going on around me, in a sort of stupor, utterly crushed over the horrors about me. I do not know how long I had lain there, perhaps ten minutes, perhaps half an hour, when suddenly I heard a gruff, deep voice behind me — the brigadier, who had come around to inspect and to give orders about the outposts. His calm, quiet voice brought me to my senses and I reported to him. His self-assurance, kindness, and determination dominated the situation. Within five minutes he had restored confidence, giving definite orders for the welfare of every one, man and beast alike, showing his solicitude for the wounded, for the sick and weak ones, and mingling praise and admonition in just measure. As by magic I felt fortified. Here was a real man undaunted by nervous qualms or by over-sensitiveness. The horrors of the war were distasteful to him, but he bore them with equanimity. It was, perhaps, the first time in my life that I regretted that my artistic education had over-sharpened and over-strung my nervous system, when I saw how manfully and bravely that man bore what seemed to me almost unbearable. His whole machinery of thinking was not complicated and not for a moment did qualms of "Weltschmerz" or exaggerated altruism burden his conscience and interfere with his straight line of conduct which was wholly determined by duty and code of honor. In his private life he was an unusually kind man. His solicitude for his subordinates, for prisoners, and for the wounded was touching, yet he saw the horrors of the war unflinchingly and without weakening, for were they not the consequences of the devotion of men to their cause? The whole thing seemed quite natural to him. The man was clearly in his element and dominated it.

After having inspected the outposts, I went back, bedded myself in a soft sand-heap, covered myself up, and was soon fast and peacefully asleep. During the night the dew moistened the sand, and when I awoke in the morning I found myself encased in a plastering which could not be removed for days.

III

OUR hopes of getting a little rest and respite from the fighting were soon scattered, for a scouting aeroplane brought news that the Russians were again advancing in overwhelming strength. Our commanding general, coming to the conclusion that with the reduced and weakened forces at his command he could not possibly offer any effective resistance to a renewed onslaught, had determined to fall back slowly before their pressure. The consequence was a series of retreating battles for us, which lasted about ten days and which constituted what is now called the battle of Lemberg.

We were then terribly outnumbered by the Russians, and in order to extricate our army and prevent it from being surrounded and cut off, we constantly had to retreat, one detachment taking up positions to resist the advancing Russians, trying to hold them at all costs in order to give the rest of the army sufficient time to retire to safety. This maneuvering could not, of course, be carried out without the forces guarding the rear and covering the retreat suffering sometimes terrible losses.

These were depressing days, with rain and storm adding to the gloom. The men tramped wearily, hanging their heads, ashamed and humiliated by the retreat, the necessity of which they could not grasp, having, as they thought, successfully repulsed the enemy. It was difficult to make them understand that our regiment was only a cog in the huge wheel of the Austrian fighting machine and that, with a battle line extending over many miles, it was quite natural that partial successes could take place and yet the consideration of general strategy necessitate a retreat. Our arguing made little impression on the men; for they only shook their heads and said, "We were victorious, we should have gone on."

The spirit of retreating troops is vastly different from that shown by an advancing army, and it was probably in recognition of this well-known psychological state that our general staff had in the beginning attacked the Russians wherever they could, in spite of the overwhelming superiority of the foe, but the reinforcements the Russians were able to draw upon had swelled their ranks so enormously that any attack would have been little short of madness.

The real hardships and privations for us began only now. The few roads of Galicia, which at best are in bad condition, through the constant passing of heavy artillery and wagons of all kinds following each other in endless proces-

Supply train moving into Russia

A halt during an infantry advance

sion through constant rains, had become well-nigh impassable, the heavy mud constituting an additional impediment to the marching of troops. In order to get all of the train carrying provisions out of the possible reach of a sudden raid by the Russian cavalry, it had to be sent miles back of us, so as not to interfere with the movement of the troops. This caused somewhat of an interruption in the organization of the commissary department and very little food reached the troops, and that only at very long intervals.

The distribution of food to an army, even in peace and under the best conditions, is a very complicated and difficult undertaking. Provisions are shipped from the interior to the important railway centers, which serve as huge army depots and form the basis from which the different army corps draw their provisions and from which they are constantly replenished. They in turn supply the divisions and brigades wherefrom the regiments and battalions draw their provisions. So it is seen that the great aorta which leads from the interior to the big depots slowly subdivides itself into smaller arteries and feeders until they reach the ultimate destination, the extreme front.

This distribution of food had now become a formidable task, in consequence of the unforeseen movements and diversions which were forced upon us by the unexpected developments of the battle; and it often happened that food supplies intended for a certain detachment would reach their destination only after the departure of that detachment.

My platoon had by this time shrunk from fifty-five men to about thirty-four, but those remaining had become very hardened, efficient, and fit. It is astonishing how quickly the human organism adjusts itself, if need be, to the most difficult circumstances. So far as I was concerned, for instance, I adapted myself to the new life without any trouble at all, responding to the unusual demands upon me automatically, as it were. My rather impaired eyesight improved in the open, with only wide distances to look at. I found that my muscles served me better than ever before. I leaped and ran and supported fatigue that would have appalled me under other circumstances. In the field all neurotic symptoms seem to disappear as by magic, and one's whole system is charged with energy and vitality. Perhaps this is due to the open-air life with its simplified standards, freed from all the complex exigencies of society's laws, and unhampered by conventionalities, as well as to the constant throb of excitement, caused by the activity, the adventure, and the uncertainty of fate.

The very massing together of so many individuals, with every will merged into one that strives with gigantic effort toward a common end, and the consequent simplicity and directness of all purpose, seem to release and unhinge all the primitive, aboriginal forces stored in the human soul, and tend to create the indescribable atmosphere of exultation which envelopes everything and everybody as with a magic cloak.

It is extraordinary how quickly suggestions of luxury, culture, refinement, in fact all the gentler aspects of life, which one had considered to be an integral part of one's life are quickly forgotten, and, more than that, not even missed. Centuries drop from one, and one becomes a primeval man, nearing the cave-dweller in an incredibly short time. For twenty-one days I went without taking off my clothes, sleeping on wet grass or in mud, or in the swamps, wherever need be, and with nothing but my cape to cover me. Nothing disturbs one. One night, while sleeping, we were drenched to the skin by torrential rains. We never stirred, but waited for the sun to dry us out again. Many things considered necessities of civilization simply drop out of existence. A toothbrush was not imaginable. We ate instinctively, when we had food, with our hands. If we had stopped to think of it at all, we should have thought it ludicrous to use knife and fork.

We were all looking like shaggy, lean wolves, from the necessity of subsisting on next to nothing. I remember having gone for more than three days at a time without any food whatsoever, and many a time we had to lick the dew from the grass for want of water. A certain fierceness arises in you, an absolute indifference to anything the world holds except your duty of fighting. You are eating a crust of bread, and a man is shot dead in the trench next to you. You look calmly at him for a moment, and then go on eating your bread. Why not? There is nothing to be done. In the end you talk of your own death with as little excitement as you would of a luncheon engagement. There is nothing left in your mind but the fact that hordes of men to whom you belong are fighting against other hordes, and your side must win.

My memory of these days is very much blurred, every day being pretty nearly the same as the preceding one, — fatiguing marches, little rest and comparatively little fighting.

It is quite possible that our commander tried to divide the work of the troops in a just manner, and that in consequence of my regiment having borne the brunt of two terrible attacks, and having suffered considerable loss, we were now temporarily withdrawn from the fighting line, and not once during these days were assigned to the duty of a rear guard. Consequently we had only few and unimportant skirmishes in these days, twice while guarding the flank through having to repulse attacks of Cossacks, and once being harrassed by an armored automobile. But the movements of an automobile being confined to the road, we had no difficulty in avoiding its fire, and as for the Cossacks with their eternal feigned attacks, we had reached the point where we almost ignored them.

We were in the first days of September, and upon reaching the swamps near Grodeck, south of Lemberg, a determined stand was decided upon by our commanding general. It seemed the most propitious place for a formidable defense, there being only few roads through otherwise impassable swamps. On September sixth my battalion was ordered to take up a position commanding a defile which formed one of the possible approaches for the enemy. Here we awaited the Russians, and they were not long in coming. First they violently shelled our position and silenced one of our batteries. Finding their artillery fire did not draw any answer from our side, they attempted to storm our position by means of frontal infantry attacks, combined with occasional raids of Cossacks, which were always repulsed. Finally the Russian infantry succeeded in establishing a number of trenches, the one opposite us not more than five hundred yards away. It was the first time we had come in close touch with the Russians, almost within hailing distance, and with the aid of our field glasses we could occasionally even get a glimpse of their faces and recognize their features. We stayed four days opposite each other, neither side gaining a foot of ground.

FOUR WEEKS IN THE TRENCHES

It was there and then that I made a curious observation. After the second day we had almost grown to know each other. The Russians would laughingly call over to us, and the Austrians would answer. The salient feature of these three days' fighting was the extraordinary lack of hatred. In fact, it is astonishing how little actual hatred exists between fighting men. One fights fiercely and passionately, mass against mass, but as soon as the mass crystallizes itself into human individuals whose features one actually can recognize, hatred almost ceases. Of course, fighting continues, but somehow it loses its fierceness and takes more the form of a sport, each side being eager to get the best of the other. One still shoots at his opponent, but almost regrets when he sees him drop.

By the morning of the third day we knew nearly every member of the opposing trench, the favorite of my men being a giant red-bearded Russian whose constant pastime consisted in jumping like a Jack-in-the-box from the trench, crying over to us as he did so. He was frequently shot at, but never hit. Then he grew bolder, showing himself longer and longer, until finally he jumped out of the trench altogether, shouting to us wildly and waving his cap. His good-humored jollity and bravado appealed to our boys and none of them attempted to shoot at him while he presented such a splendid target. Finally one of our men, who did not want to be second in bravery, jumped out of the trench and presented himself in the full sunlight. Not one attempt was made to shoot at him either, and these two men began to gesticulate at each other, inviting each other to come nearer. All fighting had suddenly ceased, and both opposing parties were looking on, laughing like boys at play. Finally the Russian would draw a step nearer, and our man boldly advanced too. Then the Russians urged on their man with shouts and laughter, and he made a big leap forward, standing still, whereupon the Austrian also jumped forward, and so, step by step, they approached until they nearly touched each other. They had left their rifles behind, and we thought that they were going to indulge in a fist fight, all of us being sorry for our champion, for he was a small and insignificant-looking man who looked as if he could be crushed with one blow by his gigantic opponent. But lo, and behold! The big Russian held out his hand which held a package of tobacco and our Austrian, seizing the tobacco, grasped the hand of the Russian, and then reaching in his pocket produced a long Austrian cigar, which he ceremoniously presented to the Russian. It was indeed a funny sight to see the small, wiry, lean Austrian talking in exaggerated terms of politeness to the blond Russian giant, who listened gravely and attentively, as if he understood every word.

By this time all precautions and even ideas of fighting had been forgotten, and we were surprised to find ourselves out of the shelter of our trenches and fully exposed to the Russians, who, in turn, leaned out of their own trenches and showed their heads in full. This unofficial truce had lasted about twenty minutes, and succeeded more in restoring good humor and joy of life among our soldiers than a trainload of provisions would have done. It was one of the incidents that helped to relieve the monotony of trench life and was heartily welcomed by all of us. The fighting, however, soon was resumed with all its earnestness and fierceness, but from this moment on a certain *camaraderie* was established between the two opposing trenches. Between skirmishes an unofficial truce would frequently be called for the purpose of removing the wounded. During these times when the stretcher-bearers were busy, no shot would be fired on either side.

Nor was this an isolated case, for similar intermittent truces, sometimes accompanied by actual intercourse between the opposing forces, were quite common all along the battle line. That very night I was hurriedly summoned to the trenches of the 13th Company, about half a mile east of us, in order to act as an interpreter between the major commanding that battalion and two singular guests he had just received, a Russian officer and his orderly. The pair, carrying a white flag, had hailed one of the numerous Austrian outposts placed during the night, in front of the trenches, and had been sent blindfolded back to the major. The Russian officer spoke only broken French. He commanded one of the opposing trenches, and from his narrative it appeared that his men had not received any food supplies for some days and were actually on the point of starvation. Not being able to stand their misery any longer, he had taken the bull by the horns and, with the utter confidence and straightforwardness of a fearless nature, had simply come over to us, the enemy, for help, offering a little barrel of water which his companion carried on his head and a little tobacco, in exchange for some provisions.

The major seemed at first, perhaps, a little perplexed and undecided about this singular request, but his generous nature and chivalry soon asserted itself. One single look at the emaciated and worn faces of our guests sufficiently substantiated the truth of their story, for both men were utterly exhausted and on the verge of collapse. The next minute messengers were flying to the different trenches of the battalion to solicit and collect contributions, and the officers scrambled over each other in their noble contest to deplete their own last and cherished reserves for the supper of the guests. Soon the latter were seated as comfortably as circumstances permitted before a feast of canned beef, cheese, biscuits, and a slice of salami, my own proud contribution consisting of two tablets of chocolate, part of a precious reserve for extreme cases. It was a strange sight to see these two Russians in an Austrian trench, surrounded by cordiality and tender solicitude. The big brotherhood of humanity had for the time enveloped friend and foe, stamping out all hatred and racial differences. It is wonderful how the most tender flowers of civilization can go hand in hand with the most brutal atrocities of grim modern warfare.

In the mean while the messengers had returned almost staggering under the weight of a sack filled with the gifts of our soldiers to the enemy, — pieces of bread and biscuits with here and there a slice of bacon or a lump of cheese, all thrown *pêle-mêle* together. Many a man must have parted with his last piece of bread in order not to be outdone by the others in generosity, for our own provisions were running very low. It is true that the bread and biscuits were mildewed, the cheese stale, and the bacon as hard as stone, but the boys gave the best they could, the very poverty and humbleness of the gifts attesting their own desperate plight, and bearing proud witness to the extent of their sacrifice. With tears in their eyes and reiterated protestations of thanks, our guests staggered back through the night to their lines, undoubtedly carrying with them tender memories of Austrian generosity and hospitality.

On the morning of the next day a Russian detachment succeeded in storming a hill on our flank, commanding the strip of space between ourselves and our reserves in the rear, thus cutting us off from our main body. They established there a machine-gun battery, and, although we were under cover in our trench, we were now in a very precarious position, for no more provisions or ammunition could reach us, all attempts to do so breaking down under a terrific machine-gun fire, but we had orders to hold our position at all cost and to the last man. Unfortunately our ammunition was giving out, in spite of our husbanding it as much as possible and shooting only when we had a sure target. The Russians soon found that each shot meant a victim and took no chances on showing even the tips of their caps. Neither could we move the least bit without being the target for a volley from their side. Up to this day I cannot understand why they did not try to rush us, but apparently they were unaware of our comparative weakness.

Also for another reason our position had become more and more untenable. We were on swampy ground and the water was constantly oozing in from the bottom of the trench, so that we sometimes had to stand nearly knee-deep and were forced to bail the water out with our caps. It is difficult to imagine a more deplorable situation than to have to stay for four days in a foul trench, half filled with swamp water, constantly exposed to the destructive fire of the enemy, utterly isolated and hopeless.

Soon we were completely without any food or water and our ammunition was almost exhausted. During the night, here and there daring men would rush through the space swept by the Russian gun fire, which was kept up constantly, trying to bring us what scanty supplies they could procure from neighboring trenches better provided than we were, but the little they brought was nothing compared to our needs.

On the evening of that third day, knowing that our ammunition was giving out, we felt that the next day would bring the end, and all our thoughts turned homewards and to the dear ones. We all wrote what we considered our parting and last farewell, each one pledging himself to deliver and take care of the letters of the others if he survived. It was a grave, sad, deeply touching moment, when we resigned ourselves to the inevitable, and yet somehow we all felt relieved and satisfied that the end might come and grimly resolved to sell our lives dearly.

Never before had I as much reason to admire the wonderful power of endurance and stoicism of our soldiers as on that night. Once resigned to the worst, all the old-time spirit returned, as if by magic. They sat together playing cards in as much moonlight as would fall into the deep trench, relating jokes and bolstering up one another's courage.

The fourth day broke gloomy, with a drizzling rain. At ten o'clock one of our men became suddenly insane, jumped out of the trench, danced wildly and divested himself of every stitch of clothing while doing so. Strange to say, the Russians must have realized that the man was insane, for they never fired at him, neither did they at the two men who jumped out to draw him back. We succeeded in comforting and subduing him, and he soon fell into a stupor and remained motionless for some time. As soon as darkness fell we succeeded in conveying him back to the reserves and I understand that he got quite well again in a few days.

At five o'clock that afternoon we suddenly received orders through a running messenger, who was braving the incessant machine-gun fire, that our positions were about to be abandoned and that we were to evacuate our trench under the cover of darkness, at eleven o'clock. I cannot but confess that we all breathed more freely on the receipt of that information, but unfortunately the purpose could not be carried out. The Russians by this time evidently had realized our comparatively defenseless condition and utter lack of ammunition, for that same night we heard two shots ring out, being a signal from our sentinels that they were surprised and that danger was near. I hardly had time to draw my sword, to grasp my revolver with my left hand and issue a command to my men to hold their bayonets in readiness, when we heard a tramping of horses and saw dark figures swooping down upon us. For once the Cossacks actually carried out their attack, undoubtedly owing to their intimate knowledge of our lack of ammunition. My next sensation was a crushing pain in my shoulder, struck by the hoof of a horse, and a sharp knife pain in my right thigh. I fired with my revolver at the hazy figure above me, saw it topple over and then lost consciousness.

This happened, to the best of my recollection, at about half past ten at night. Upon coming to my senses I found my faithful orderly, kneeling in the trench by my side. He fairly shouted with delight as I opened my eyes. According to his story the Austrians, falling back under the cavalry charge, had evacuated the trench without noticing, in the darkness, that I was missing. But soon discovering my absence he started back to the trench in search of me. It was a perilous undertaking for him, for the Cossacks were still riding about, and he showed me with pride the place where a stray bullet had perforated his knapsack during the search. He revived me, gave me first aid, and succeeded with great difficulty in helping me out of the trench. For more than three hours we stumbled on in the night, trying to find our lines again. Twice we encountered a small troop of Cossacks, but upon hearing the tramping we quietly lay down on the wayside without a motion until they had passed. Happily we were not noticed by them, and from then we stumbled on without any further incident until we were hailed by an Austrian outpost and in safety. By this time I was utterly exhausted and again lost consciousness.

When I opened my eyes, I was in a little hut where our ambulance gave first aid. Therefrom I was transported to the nearest field hospital. This, however, had to be broken up and the wounded removed because of the Russian advance. We were hastily put on big ambulance wagons without springs, the jolting of which over the bad road caused us such suffering that we should have almost preferred to walk or crawl. We tried to reach the railway station at Komarno but found a Russian detachment had intercepted us. In the streets of the village a shell burst almost in front of our wagons, making the horses shy and causing a great deal of confusion. We had to turn back and after a long and wearisome detour reached our destination, the troop hospital in Sambor, in a state of great exhaustion. There I remained but a day. The less seriously wounded had to make place for the graver cases, and being among the former, I was transferred by hospital train to Miscolcy in Hungary. The same crowded conditions prevailed here as in Sambor, and after a night's rest I again was put on board a Red

Troops arriving back home

Returning soldiers at the Brandenburg Gate, Berlin

Cross train en route to Vienna. We were met at the station by a number of Red Cross nurses and assistant doctors.

To my great joy my wife was among the former, having been assigned to that particular duty. A short official telegram to the effect that I was being sent home wounded on hospital train Number 16 was the first news she had received about me for fully four weeks. None of my field postcards had arrived and she was suffering extreme nervous strain from the long anxiety and suspense, which she had tried in vain to numb by feverish work in her hospital. I remained two weeks in Vienna and then was transferred to the sulphur bath of Baden near-by, where large hospitals had been established to relieve the overcrowding of Vienna. There I remained until the first of November when I was ordered to appear before a mixed commission of army surgeons and senior officers, for a medical examination. Two weeks later I received formal intimation that I had been pronounced invalid and physically unfit for army duty at the front or at home, and consequently was exempted from further service. My military experience ended there, and with deep regret I bade good-bye to my loyal brother officers, comrades, and faithful orderly, and discarded my well-beloved uniform for the nondescript garb of the civilian, grateful that I had been permitted to be of any, if ever so little, service to my Fatherland.

THE END

Fritz Kreisler as an officer in the Austrian Reserve and his wife Harriet as a nurse.

Rear endpapers:
A   World War I
infantry advance.